BLOODTHIRSTY PLANTS

AN IMAGINATION LIBRARY SERIES

PITCHER PLANTS
Slippery Pits of No Escape

By Victor Gentle

With special thanks to the people at
the Carolina Biological Supply Company,
and to Ms. Chiaki Shibata,
for their kind encouragement and help.

Gareth Stevens Publishing
MILWAUKEE

For a free color catalog describing Gareth Stevens' list of high-quality books and multimedia programs, call 1-800-542-2595 (USA) or 1-800-461-9120 (Canada). Gareth Stevens Publishing's Fax: (414) 225-0377. See our catalog, too, on the World Wide Web: http://gsinc.com

Library of Congress Cataloging-in-Publication Data

Gentle, Victor.
  Pitcher plants: slippery pits of no escape / by Victor Gentle.
    p. cm. — (Bloodthirsty plants)
  Includes bibliographical references (p. 23) and index.
  Summary: Introduces these carnivorous plants by describing their traps, plant types, diet, and nutrient-poor habitats with the consequent benefit of carnivory.
    ISBN 0-8368-1657-9 (lib. bdg.)
  1. Pitcher plants–Juvenile literature. [1. Pitcher plants. 2. Carnivorous plants.] I. Title.
II. Series: Gentle, Victor. Bloodthirsty plants.
  QK917.G46 1996
  583'.121–dc20   96-5607

First published in 1996 by
Gareth Stevens Publishing
1555 North RiverCenter Drive, Suite 201
Milwaukee, WI 53212 USA

Text: Victor Gentle
Page layout: Victor Gentle and Karen Knutson
Cover design: Karen Knutson
Photo credits: Cover (main), p. 13 (both) © Carolina Biological Supply Company; cover (background) © Stuart Wasserman/Picture Perfect; pp. 5, 7, 9, 11 © Visuals Unlimited/Kjell B. Sandved; p. 15 © Ken W. Davis/Tom Stack & Associates; pp. 17, 19 © Chiaki Shibata; p. 21 © Jo-Ann Ordano/PHOTO/NATS

Printed in the United States of America

1 2 3 4 5 6 7 8 9 01 00 99 98 97 96

TABLE OF CONTENTS

THE PIT OF NO ESCAPE

In the highlands of tropical Borneo, it is a hot, sultry afternoon. The cries of birds and monkeys and the buzz of insects fill the air. So does the sweet smell of an unusual kind of plant. From the jungle canopy, at the end of half a dozen vines, hang strange and colorful jugs, or pitchers. The jugs have blood-red lips.

A large flying insect lands on the rim of one of the jugs. Just inside the lip, a sweet **nectar** attracts the insect. The insect moves forward and down. Inside the rim, the smooth surface offers no foothold. Within a few seconds, the unlucky insect loses its footing and tumbles in. There is no escape.

A tropical pitcher plant from Indonesia waits for a meal. This *Nepenthes* (nuh-PEN-theez) is a natural **hybrid**, a cross between a lowland pitcher plant and a highland pitcher plant.

MONKEY CUPS

The insect has been trapped by a **carnivorous** pitcher plant, a plant that eats animals! This plant belongs to the **genus** Nepenthes. Nepenthes live in the **humid** jungles of Madagascar, Sri Lanka, the countries and islands of Southeast Asia, and the northern tip of Australia. There are more than seventy **species** of Nepenthes worldwide, none of which grow wild in Europe or the Americas.

Some Nepenthes have traps so big that small birds, frogs, and rodents can fall in and be eaten. Even small monkeys have been known to fall into the biggest traps! But that is not why the Nepenthes are commonly known as monkey cups.

They are called monkey cups because large jungle apes, such as orangutans, actually hold them up and drink from them. No kidding.

Nepenthes lowii (LOE-ee-ee), a tropical pitcher plant with one of the largest traps in the business! It is easy to see how a small monkey might fall into it.

DROWNING AND DISSOLVING

The bases of the pitchers are filled with rainwater. After the victim tumbles in, **glands** on the inside of the pitcher release **acids** and **enzymes** to **digest** the soft, nutritious parts. Within a few hours, all but the wings and skeleton of the victim have been dissolved and absorbed by the plant. Some larger insects and small animals may take longer to digest — a few days, perhaps.

Like all other kinds of carnivorous pitcher plants, monkey cups grow in poor soil. The bodies of insects and other small animals give these plants the **nutrients** they need.

Many *Nepenthes* make two kinds of traps. The hanging traps catch flying **prey**. The ground-level traps catch crawling or jumping prey.

A pitcher trap of a tropical pitcher plant, cut open to show insect remains . . . and a spider that made the trap its home. Now, why would a spider want to make its home inside a carnivorous plant?

THE ALBANY PITCHER PLANT

Like the monkey cup, the Albany pitcher plant has traps with narrow, partly-capped openings. Unlike the monkey cup, this genus has only one species — *Cephalotus follicularis* (seff-uh-LOH-tus fuh-LIK-yoo-LAHR-iss). This species is only found along a 150-mile (240-kilometer)-wide coastal strip of southwestern Australia.

The traps are small, growing only 2 to 3 inches (5 to 8 centimeters) high. They are hairy on the outside, making it easy for all kinds of crawling insects to climb up to the rim. The wide rim is covered with sharp, inward-facing teeth. These teeth stop insects from climbing out.

Albany pitcher plants also capture many flying insects. But the plants' favorite food is . . . ants.

Albany pitcher plants, first discovered by French explorers in 1792. The traps are green in normal light, but turn a beautiful deep red or purple in strong sunshine.

TRUMPET PITCHERS OF NORTH AMERICA

There are eight species of trumpet pitchers, or *Sarracenia* (sar-ra-SEE-nyuh). They grow in central and southeastern Canada, and in the eastern United States.

Sarracenia traps are special kinds of leaves. People often think the traps are flowers because they look pretty. Flies, bees, wasps, and many other insects make the same mistake! They are attracted by the colors of the leaves and the sweet smell.

Near the lips, short hairs make it easy for an insect to keep a grip. But as the insect crawls inside, the hairs point downward. It is hard to climb back. Farther inside, the surface is smooth. Insects can't help but slip to the bottom. There they drown and dissolve in the digestive juices of the plant.

A northern pitcher plant, *Sarracenia purpurea* (per-per-REE-yuh), with a captured cricket (*top picture*) and cut open (*bottom picture*) to show insect remains.

THE COBRA LILY

Cobra lilies grow in the mountains of northern California and western Oregon. The cobra lily is the only species in the genus *Darlingtonia* (dar-ling-TOE-nyuh). It is a close relative of the trumpet pitchers. Its pitcher traps are like those of the trumpet pitchers. They are similar in shape, in the way they work, and in the way they trap and digest insects. But the flowers are quite different. That is why **botanists** put the cobra lily in a separate genus. Its species name is *Darlingtonia californica* (cal-luh-FOR-nik-uh).

Cobra lilies eat small and large insects. Beetles, bees, butterflies, cockroaches, dragonflies, and grasshoppers all provide good meals. Cobra lilies even catch and eat small snails.

Darlingtonia californica, or cobra lilies, growing in the wild. The first European to "discover" cobra lilies found them on Mt. Shasta, California, in 1841. They were known to American Indians long before.

THE RARE SUN PITCHERS

The six species of sun pitchers, or *Heliamphora* (hee-lee-AM-for-uh), are found only in the remote Roraima Mountains in South America. These mountains are where the countries of Venezuela, Brazil, and Guyana meet. Sun pitchers all have green to red tubelike pitcher traps.

Sun pitchers live on high, marshy **plateaus** between 3,000 and 10,000 feet (1,000 to 3,000 meters) high. These sandstone plateaus, called *tepuis*, were formed about 1,600 million years ago.

The first European to see and study them was the British explorer, Sir Robert Schomburgk, in 1839.

Most of the time, sun pitchers live under clear skies and very bright sunlight. The pitchers' colors and sweet nectar attract insects to their doom.

A group of sun pitchers, *Heliamphora nutans* (NYOO-tanz), growing in the wild at Mt. Cuquenán Matawi Tepuy, near Mt. Roraima in Venezuela.

A SURPRISE INSIDE!

Another plant genus found on the *tepuis* and on surrounding lowland marshes of Venezuela is *Brocchinia* (bruh-KIN-yuh). This genus was discovered and named more than 160 years ago. But it was only in 1984 that botanists realized that two of the five *Brocchinia* species are carnivorous.

Like the trumpet pitchers, the cobra lilies, and the sun pitchers, *Brocchinia* have trumpet-shaped pitchers. The two carnivorous *Brocchinia* are so rare that they have no common names, just scientific names: *Brocchinia reducta* (ruh-DUK-tuh) and *Brocchinia hectioides* (HEK-tee-O-uh-deez).

Brocchinia reducta holds another surprise. Another carnivorous plant often grows between its leaves — a bladderwort, a plant with tiny, vacuum-like traps.

One carnivorous plant inside another! See the round, green leaves. They belong to the bladderwort *Utricularia humboldtii* (yoo-TRIK-yoo-LAH-ryuh hum-BOLE-tee-eye), growing out from between the leaves of *Brocchinia reducta*, growing wild on Mt. Huachamacari in Venezuela.

THE WORLD OF CARNIVOROUS PLANTS

The pitcher plants in this book all use a "pitfall" trap. Other carnivorous plants use different "tricks of the trade."

Venus fly traps catch insects with incredibly fast spring traps. The sundews trap insects on sweet, sticky tentacles. Once caught, victims cannot struggle free. Other carnivorous plants, the butterworts, catch their prey on greasy, oozing leaves. Yet others, the bladderworts, act like vacuum cleaners, sucking in small insects and tiny fish. Some carnivorous **fungi** even lasso their prey!

You can learn more about the strange and wonderful world of carnivorous plants by reading other books. You can also learn more by getting your own plants and watching them grow.

This tropical pitcher plant, a *Nepenthes balmy koto* (BAL-mee KOE-toe), is a hybrid not found in the wild. It was crossbred in California from a Vietnamese *Nepenthes* and an Indonesian *Nepenthes*. The back lighting shows the shadows of hundreds of ants trapped inside one of its pitchers.

GROWING PITCHER PLANTS YOURSELF

Some pitcher plants are easy to grow. Many tropical pitcher plants need to be kept at higher temperatures. Others live naturally in highland country where it can get quite cool. Some *Sarracenia* can even survive freezing weather.

It's best to get specific instructions about the plants from the people who supply them.

WHERE TO GET PLANTS OR SEEDS

Here are some addresses of carnivorous plant suppliers. For other sources, contact a club or society listed on the next page.

Sarracenia Nurseries
Links Side, Courtland Avenue, Mill Hill
London NW7 3BG England

Carolina Biological Supply Company
2700 York Road
Burlington, NC 27215 USA

Peter Paul's Nursery
4665 Chapin Road
Canandaigua, NY 14424 USA

Exotica Plants
Community Mail Bag
Cordalba QLD 4660 Australia

Hillier Water Gardens
Box 662, Qualicum Beach
BC V9K 1T2 Canada

Silverhill Seeds
P.O. Box 53108, Kenilworth 7745
Republic of South Africa

Carolina Exotic Gardens
Route 5, Box 283-A
Greenville, NC 27834 USA

California Carnivores
7020 Trenton-Healdsburg Road
Forestville, CA 95436 USA

MORE TO READ AND VIEW

Books (nonfiction):   *Bladderworts: Trapdoors to Oblivion.* Victor Gentle (Gareth Stevens)
                                      Butterworts: Greasy Cups of Death. Victor Gentle (Gareth Stevens)
                                      Carnivorous Mushrooms: Lassoing their Prey? Victor Gentle (Gareth Stevens)
                                      Carnivorous Plants. Nancy J. Nielsen (Franklin Watts)
                                      Killer Plants. Mycol Doyle (Lowell House Juvenile)
                                      Pitcher Plants: The Elegant Insect Traps. Carol Lerner (Morrow)
                                      Plants of Prey. Densey Clyne (Gareth Stevens)
                                      Sundews: A Sweet and Sticky Death. Victor Gentle (Gareth Stevens)
                                      Venus Fly Traps and Waterwheels. Victor Gentle (Gareth Stevens)
Books (fiction):   *Elizabite: Adventures of a Carnivorous Plant.* H.A. Rey (Linnet)
                                      Island of Doom. Richard Brightfield (Gareth Stevens)
Videos (nonfiction):   *Carnivorous Plants.* (Oxford Scientific Films)
Videos (fiction):   *The Day of the Triffids* and *The Little Shop of Horrors* are fun to watch.

WHERE TO WRITE TO FIND OUT MORE

Your community may have a local chapter of a carnivorous plant society. Try looking it up in the telephone directory. Or contact one of the following national organizations:

Australia
Australian Carnivorous Plant Society, Inc.
P.O. Box 391
St. Agnes, South Australia 5097 Australia

New Zealand
New Zealand Carnivorous Plant Society
P.O. Box 21-381, Henderson
Auckland, New Zealand

United Kingdom
The Carnivorous Plant Society
174 Baldwins Lane, Croxley Green
Hertfordshire WD3 3LQ
England

Canada
Eastern Carnivorous Plant Society
Dionaea, 23 Cherryhill Drive
Grimsby, Ontario, Canada L3M 3B3

South Africa – has no CP society, but
a supplier to contact is:
Eric Green, 11 Wepener Street
Southfield, 7800, Cape, South Africa

United States
International Carnivorous Plant Society
Fullerton Arboretum
California State University at Fullerton
Fullerton, CA 92634 USA

If you are on the Internet, or otherwise on-line, you can call up a World Wide Web page that gives links to other Web pages of interest to carnivorous plant enthusiasts: http://www.cvp.com/feedme/links.html

GLOSSARY

You can find these words on the pages listed. Reading a word in a sentence helps you understand it even better.

acids (ASS-ids) — harsh liquids that can dissolve many things 8

botanists (BOT-uh-nists) — scientists who study plants 14, 18

carnivorous (kar-NIV-er-us) — flesh-eating 6, 8, 16, 18, 20

digest (die-JEST) — to break into bits that the body can use for food 8

enzymes (EN-zimes) — special substances that help digestion 8

fungi (FUN-JYE) — the plural of **fungus** — a fungus is a plant without the green substance found in most leafy plants, so it can't make its own food from sunlight, air, and water 20

genus (JEE-nus) — a group of closely related plants or animals 6, 14, 18

glands (GLANZ) — special plant parts that produce and absorb liquid substances 8

humid (HYOO-mid) — damp 6

hybrid (HI-brid) — a cross between two species 4, 20

nectar (NEK-ter) — a sweet, sugary substance 4, 16

nutrients (NOO-tree-unts) — substances with good food value 8

plateaus (pla-TOES) — high, flat pieces of land 16

prey (PRAY) — a victim of a hunter, trapper, or trap 8, 20

species (SPEE-shees) — an individual type of plant or animal 6, 10, 12, 14, 16, 18

INDEX